THE SUPREME
NEWYORK JETS
TRIVIA AND QUIZBOOK

BY: JACKSON WELLS

© Copyright 2023-All rights reserved.

The content contained within this book may not be reproduced, duplicated, or transmitted without direct written permission from the author or the publisher.

Under no circumstances will any blame or legal responsibility be held against the publisher, or author, for any damages, reparation, or monetary loss due to the information contained within this book, either directly or indirectly.

Legal Notice:

This book is copyright protected. It is only for personal use. You cannot amend, distribute, sell, use, quote, or paraphrase any part, or the content within this book, without the consent of the author or publisher.

Disclaimer Notice:

Please note the information contained within this document is for educational and entertainment purposes only.

Table of Contents

- INTRODUCTION TO NEWYORK JETS 5
- HISTORY 6
  - QUESTION TIME! 6
  - ANSWERS 16
- TEAM HISTORY 18
  - QUESTION TIME! 18
  - ANSWERS 28
- HOME STADIUM 30
  - QUESTION TIME! 30
  - ANSWERS 40
- RIVALRIES 42
  - QUESTION TIME! 42
  - ANSWERS 53
- COACHING LEGENDS 55
  - QUESTION TIME! 55
  - ANSWERS 65
- JETS IN THE PLAYOFFS 68
  - QUESTION TIME! 68
  - ANSWERS 79
- COMMUNITY ENGAGEMENT 81
  - QUESTION TIME! 81
  - ANSWERS 92
- FUTURE PROSPECTS 95
  - QUESTION TIME! 95
  - ANSWERS 104

GRAET PLAYERS IN JETS HISTORY 107
   QUESTION TIME! 107
   ANSWERS 117

INTRODUCTION TO NEWYORK JETS

As the New York Jets celebrate their illustrious history and mark another year in the NFL, the iconic green and white colors continue to symbolize a legacy of passion, resilience, and determination. Over the past year, the Jets have navigated the gridiron with fervor, showcasing the indomitable spirit that defines this storied franchise. From thrilling victories to hard-fought challenges, the team's journey is etched in the hearts of fans and woven into the tapestry of New York sports lore. As they embark on a new season, the Jets stand ready to carve out their destiny, fueled by the unwavering support of their dedicated fan base and the echoes of triumphs past that resonate throughout the hallowed halls of MetLife Stadium.

HISTORY
QUESTION TIME!

1. Who is the all-time leading passer in New York Jets history?

   a. Joe Namath

   b. Ken O'Brien

   c. Chad Pennington

   d. Mark Sanchez

2. Which player holds the record for the most rushing yards in a single season for the New York Jets?

   a. Curtis Martin

   b. Freeman McNeil

   c. Thomas Jones

   d. Bilal Powell

3. The New York Jets won their first and only Super Bowl in which year?

   a. 1968

   b. 1972

   c. 1981

   d. 1994

4. Who is the all-time leading receiver in terms of receiving yards for the New York Jets?

   a. Don Maynard

   b. Wesley Walker

   c. Al Toon

   d. Jerricho Cotchery

5. In what round of the NFL Draft was Joe Namath selected by the New York Jets?

   a. 1st

   b. 2nd

   c. 3rd

   d. 4th

6. Which coach led the New York Jets to their only Super Bowl victory?

   a. Bill Parcells

   b. Weeb Ewbank

   c. Rex Ryan

   d. Herm Edwards

7. The New York Jets' home games are played at which stadium?

   a. MetLife Stadium

   b. Yankee Stadium

   c. Giants Stadium

   d. Citi Field

8. Who is known for the famous play in Super Bowl III guaranteeing a victory for the Jets?

   a. Joe Namath

   b. Matt Snell

   c. Don Maynard

   d. Emerson Boozer

9. Which defensive player is known for his iconic sack celebration, "the airplane"?

   a. Mark Gastineau

   b. Joe Klecko

   c. Shaun Ellis

   d. Muhammad Wilkerson

10. The New York Jets joined the NFL as part of the AFL-NFL merger in which year?

   a. 1960

   b. 1965

   c. 1970

   d. 1975

11. Who is the all-time leading scorer (points) in New York Jets history?

   a. Pat Leahy

   b. Nick Folk

   c. Jason Myers

   d. John Hall

12. Which player holds the record for the most interceptions in a single season for the New York Jets?

   a. Darrelle Revis

   b. Aaron Glenn

   c. Antonio Cromartie

   d. Marcus Coleman

13. The New York Jets' team colors are:

a. Green and White

b. Blue and Gold

c. Black and Silver

d. Red and White

14. Who is the youngest head coach in New York Jets history?

a. Todd Bowles

b. Rex Ryan

c. Adam Gase

d. Robert Saleh

15. The New York Jets' first regular-season game was against which team?

a. New England Patriots

b. Buffalo Bills

c. Miami Dolphins

d. Baltimore Colts

16. Which player is nicknamed "Broadway Joe"?

a. Joe Klecko

b. Joe Namath

c. Joe Ferguson

d. Joe McKnight

17. The New York Jets made history by selecting the first overall pick in the 1997 NFL Draft. Who was that player?

a. Keyshawn Johnson

b. Vinny Testaverde

c. James Farrior

d. Curtis Martin

18. In what year did the New York Jets become the first AFL team to defeat an NFL team in the Super Bowl?

a. 1967

b. 1969

c. 1973

d. 1978

19. Which quarterback succeeded Joe Namath as the starting quarterback for the New York Jets?

a. Richard Todd

b. Ken O'Brien

c. Pat Ryan

d. Tony Eason

20. The New York Jets' mascot is named:

a. Jaxson de Ville

b. Blitz

c. Fireman Ed

d. Flight Crew

21. Who is the all-time leader in sacks for the New York Jets?

a. Mark Gastineau

b. Shaun Ellis

c. Muhammad Wilkerson

d. Calvin Pace

22. The New York Jets relocated from which city to become the Jets?

a. Los Angeles

b. Baltimore

c. Houston

d. Boston

23. Which player holds the record for the most touchdown receptions in a single season for the New York Jets?

   a. Brandon Marshall

   b. Keyshawn Johnson

   c. Santana Moss

   d. Laveranues Coles

24. The New York Jets' first head coach was:

   a. Weeb Ewbank

   b. Bill Parcells

   c. Rex Ryan

   d. Lou Holtz

25. Which player was known for his memorable 108-yard kickoff return for a touchdown in Super Bowl III?

   a. George Sauer

b. Don Maynard

c. Emerson Boozer

d. Earl Christy

26. What is the name of the New York Jets' fight song?

　a. "We're the New York Jets"

　b. "Jet Power"

　c. "J-E-T-S"

　d. "Take 'Em Down"

27. Who is the only New York Jets player to win the NFL MVP award?

　a. Joe Namath

　b. Curtis Martin

　c. Vinny Testaverde

　d. Darrelle Revis

28. Which player is known for coining the term "Sack Exchange"?

　a. Joe Klecko

　b. Mark Gastineau

c. Abdul Salaam

d. Marty Lyons

29. In which year did the New York Jets move to their current home stadium, MetLife Stadium?

   a. 2007

   b. 2009

   c. 2011

   d. 2013

30. Who is the all-time leader in career interceptions for the New York Jets?

   a. Darrelle Revis

   b. Antonio Cromartie

   c. Aaron Glenn

   d. Erik McMillan

ANSWERS

1. a
2. a
3. a
4. a
5. a
6. b
7. a
8. a
9. a
10. c
11. a
12. a
13. a
14. c
15. d
16. b
17. a
18. b
19. a
20. c

21. a

22. d

23. a

24. a

25. c

26. c

27. a

28. b

29. b

30. d

TEAM HISTORY
QUESTION TIME!

1. In what year were the New York Jets founded?

    a. 1959

    b. 1960

    c. 1965

    d. 1970

2. What was the original name of the New York Jets?

    a. Titans

    b. Giants

    c. Jets

    d. Jetsam

3. Who was the first head coach of the New York Jets?

    a. Weeb Ewbank

    b. Joe Namath

    c. Don Maynard

    d. Joe Walton

4. In which year did the New York Jets win their first and only Super Bowl?

   a. 1966

   b. 1969

   c. 1972

   d. 1975

5. The famous quarterback Joe Namath played for the New York Jets from:

   a. 1965-1972

   b. 1969-1977

   c. 1970-1980

   d. 1975-1985

6. The New York Jets' home games are played at:

   a. MetLife Stadium

   b. Giants Stadium

   c. Meadowlands Stadium

   d. Jets Stadium

7. Which stadium did the New York Jets share with the New York Giants before moving to MetLife Stadium?

   a. Shea Stadium

   b. Yankee Stadium

   c. Polo Grounds

   d. Meadowlands Stadium

8. Who is the all-time leading rusher in New York Jets history?

   a. Curtis Martin

   b. Freeman McNeil

   c. Thomas Jones

   d. Emerson Boozer

9. The New York Jets are a member of which NFL division?

   a. NFC East

   b. AFC East

   c. AFC West

   d. NFC West

10. Which player famously guaranteed a victory in Super Bowl III for the New York Jets?

   a. Joe Namath

   b. Mark Sanchez

   c. Chad Pennington

   d. Ken O'Brien

11. What was the final score of Super Bowl III when the Jets defeated the Baltimore Colts?

   a. 16-7

   b. 21-17

   c. 23-20

   d. 30-27

12. The New York Jets' official mascot is named:

   a. Jumbo

   b. Blaze

   c. Swoop

   d. Flight Crew

13. In which year did the New York Jets move from Shea Stadium to Giants Stadium?

a. 1976

b. 1980

c. 1984

d. 1988

14. The New York Jets had the first overall pick in the NFL Draft in 1996 and selected:

a. Peyton Manning

b. Vinny Testaverde

c. Keyshawn Johnson

d. Bill Parcells

15. Which wide receiver holds the record for the most career receiving yards in New York Jets history?

a. Al Toon

b. Wesley Walker

c. Don Maynard

d. Wayne Chrebet

16. The New York Jets' team colors are:

a. Green and White

b. Blue and Gold

c. Black and Silver

d. Red and White

17. Who is the current head coach of the New York Jets (as of 2022)?

   a. Todd Bowles

   b. Adam Gase

   c. Robert Saleh

   d. Rex Ryan

18. In which city do the New York Jets hold their training camp?

   a. Albany, NY

   b. Florham Park, NJ

   c. Cortland, NY

   d. Hempstead, NY

19. The New York Jets' fight song is called:

   a. "J-E-T-S, Jets! Jets! Jets!"

   b. "Gang Green Glory"

c. "Green and White Pride"

d. "Jetstream Anthem"

20. Which quarterback set a franchise record for most passing touchdowns in a single season for the New York Jets?

a. Joe Namath

b. Brett Favre

c. Chad Pennington

d. Mark Sanchez

21. The New York Jets played their first season in the American Football League (AFL) before the NFL merger in:

a. 1960

b. 1965

c. 1970

d. 1975

22. Which defensive lineman is known for his famous "Namath Guarantee" in Super Bowl III?

a. Mark Gastineau

b. Joe Klecko

c. Marty Lyons

d. Abdul Salaam

23. The New York Jets' official team website is:

a. nyjets.com

b. jetsnation.com

c. greenandwhite.com

d. flightcrewcentral.com

24. Who is the all-time leader in career interceptions for the New York Jets?

a. Darrelle Revis

b. Aaron Glenn

c. Antonio Cromartie

d. Erik McMillan

25. The New York Jets' first-round pick in the 2021 NFL Draft was:

a. Zach Wilson

b. Quinnen Williams

c. Mekhi Becton

d. C.J. Mosley

26. The New York Jets' biggest rival is often considered to be:

a. New England Patriots

b. Buffalo Bills

c. Miami Dolphins

d. New York Giants

27. Which quarterback led the New York Jets to their last playoff appearance before 2021?

a. Chad Pennington

b. Mark Sanchez

c. Ryan Fitzpatrick

d. Geno Smith

28. The New York Jets retired the jersey number 12 in honor of:

a. Joe Namath

b. Don Maynard

c. Joe Klecko

d. Wayne Chrebet

29. The New York Jets won their only Super Bowl by defeating which team?

a. Dallas Cowboys

b. Green Bay Packers

c. Baltimore Colts

d. Kansas City Chiefs

30. Which player holds the record for the most career touchdowns in New York Jets history?

a. Curtis Martin

b. Don Maynard

c. Keyshawn Johnson

d. Wesley Walker

ANSWERS

1. b
2. a
3. a
4. b
5. a
6. a
7. d
8. a
9. b
10. a
11. c
12. c
13. d
14. c
15. a
16. a
17. c
18. b
19. a

20. b

21. a

22. a

23. a

24. a

25. a

26. a

27. c

28. b

29. a

30. a

HOME STADIUM
QUESTION TIME!

1. What is the name of the current home stadium of the New York Jets?

    a. MetLife Stadium

    b. Giants Stadium

    c. Meadowlands Stadium

    d. Jets Stadium

2. MetLife Stadium is located in which state?

    a. New York

    b. New Jersey

    c. Connecticut

    d. Pennsylvania

3. The construction of MetLife Stadium was completed in:

    a. 2008

b. 2010

c. 2012

d. 2014

4. MetLife Stadium is shared by the New York Jets and which other NFL team?

   a. New York Giants

   b. New England Patriots

   c. Philadelphia Eagles

   d. Dallas Cowboys

5. Before moving to MetLife Stadium, the New York Jets played their home games at:

   a. Shea Stadium

   b. Yankee Stadium

   c. Polo Grounds

   d. Giants Stadium

6. MetLife Stadium hosted Super Bowl XLVIII in which year?

   a. 2012

   b. 2014

c. 2016

d. 2018

7. Which architectural feature makes MetLife Stadium unique among NFL stadiums?

   a. Retractable Roof

   b. Circular Design

   c. Dual-purpose Video Boards

   d. Floating Field

8. The seating capacity of MetLife Stadium is approximately:

   a. 70,000

   b. 80,000

   c. 90,000

   d. 100,000

9. MetLife Stadium is situated in the Meadowlands Sports Complex, which is also home to which other major venue?

   a. Madison Square Garden

   b. Barclays Center

c. Prudential Center

d. Red Bull Arena

10. The first regular-season game at MetLife Stadium featured a matchup between the New York Jets and:

    a. New York Giants

    b. New England Patriots

    c. Dallas Cowboys

    d. Buffalo Bills

11. Which company has the naming rights for MetLife Stadium?

    a. PepsiCo

    b. MetLife, Inc.

    c. Verizon

    d. AT&T

12. The stadium hosted WrestleMania 29 in which year?

    a. 2012

    b. 2013

    c. 2014

33

d. 2015

13. MetLife Stadium has hosted concerts for which international music sensation?

   a. Beyoncé

   b. Taylor Swift

   c. U2

   d. Ed Sheeran

14. The color scheme of MetLife Stadium includes:

   a. Blue and White

   b. Green and Gold

   c. Red and Yellow

   d. Gray and Black

15. MetLife Stadium is located near which major airport?

   a. John F. Kennedy International Airport

   b. LaGuardia Airport

   c. Newark Liberty International Airport

   d. Teterboro Airport

16. The stadium's location provides a panoramic view of which iconic New York City skyline?

    a. Manhattan

    b. Brooklyn

    c. Queens

    d. The Bronx

17. MetLife Stadium hosted the Copa América Centenario Final in which year?

    a. 2015

    b. 2016

    c. 2017

    d. 2018

18. The stadium features a distinctive ring of suites and clubs known as:

    a. Skyline Suites

    b. Ring of Honor Suites

    c. Champions Club

    d. Touchdown Club

19. MetLife Stadium is often referred to as the "Home of:

   a. Champions

   b. Legends

   c. Giants and Jets

   d. Meadowlands Magic

20. The first halftime show at MetLife Stadium for a Super Bowl featured which pop music icon?

   a. Madonna

   b. Beyoncé

   c. Lady Gaga

   d. Katy Perry

21. MetLife Stadium was a host venue for the 2019 CONCACAF Gold Cup. Which sport does the Gold Cup represent?

   a. Soccer

   b. Basketball

   c. Baseball

   d. Ice Hockey

22. The stadium has a distinctive feature where fans can stand and view the game called:

   a. Fan Zone

   b. Touchdown Terrace

   c. Gridiron Gallery

   d. Four Quarters Pavilion

23. MetLife Stadium has hosted multiple editions of which major college football bowl game?

   a. Orange Bowl

   b. Sugar Bowl

   c. Cotton Bowl

   d. Pinstripe Bowl

24. The first NHL Stadium Series outdoor hockey game held at MetLife Stadium featured which teams?

   a. New York Rangers vs. New Jersey Devils

   b. Pittsburgh Penguins vs. Philadelphia Flyers

   c. Chicago Blackhawks vs. Detroit Red Wings

   d. Los Angeles Kings vs. San Jose Sharks

25. The stadium's location is adjacent to which body of water?

   a. Hudson River

   b. East River

   c. Long Island Sound

   d. Atlantic Ocean

26. The MetLife Central area inside the stadium is known for its:

   a. Fan Zone

   b. Interactive Displays

   c. VIP Lounges

   d. Outdoor Plaza

27. The first concert held at MetLife Stadium featured which legendary rock band?

   a. The Rolling Stones

   b. U2

   c. Bruce Springsteen and the E Street Band

   d. The Who

28. MetLife Stadium has hosted multiple editions of which annual college football rivalry game?

   a. Army vs. Navy

   b. Ohio State vs. Michigan

   c. Alabama vs. Auburn

   d. USC vs. Notre Dame

29. The stadium's location in the Meadowlands is known for its history of hosting events in which sport?

   a. Horse Racing

   b. Golf

   c. Tennis

   d. Auto Racing

30. MetLife Stadium is often lit up in the team colors of the:

   a. New York Giants

   b. New York Jets

   c. Both Giants and Jets

   d. New England Patriots

ANSWERS

1. a
2. b
3. b
4. a
5. d
6. b
7. c
8. b
9. c
10. a
11. b
12. b
13. c
14. d
15. c
16. a
17. b
18. c
19. c
20. c

21. a

22. a

23. d

24. b

25. a

26. b

27. a

28. a

29. a

30. c

RIVALRIES
QUESTION TIME!

1. The New York Jets' most well-known and intense rivalry is with which AFC East team?

   a. Miami Dolphins

   b. Buffalo Bills

   c. New England Patriots

   d. Indianapolis Colts

2. Which former head coach of the New York Jets famously declared, "I'm not here to kiss Bill Belichick's rings"?

   a. Rex Ryan

   b. Todd Bowles

   c. Eric Mangini

   d. Herm Edwards

3. The rivalry between the New York Jets and the New England Patriots is often referred to as:

   a. Big Apple Brawl

   b. Gotham Gridiron Clash

c. AFC East Showdown

d. Border War

4. The New York Jets and which team compete in the "Battle of New York" for local bragging rights?

   a. New York Giants

   b. Buffalo Bills

   c. Miami Dolphins

   d. New England Patriots

5. The New York Jets have a historical rivalry with the Baltimore Colts, which intensified after the famous:

   a. "Heidi Game"

   b. "Snowplow Game"

   c. "Mud Bowl"

   d. "Guarantee Game"

6. The annual matchup between the New York Jets and Miami Dolphins is known as:

   a. Empire State Showdown

   b. Sunshine Skirmish

   c. Coastal Clash

d. AFC East Derby

7. In which year did the New York Jets and the Miami Dolphins play the famous "Monday Night Miracle" game?

   a. 1997

   b. 2000

   c. 2003

   d. 2006

8. The New York Jets and the New England Patriots play for the "Jets–Patriots Trophy" in honor of:

   a. Joe Namath

   b. Bill Parcells

   c. Leon Hess

   d. Curtis Martin

9. The rivalry between the New York Jets and the New England Patriots reached its peak during the coaching tenure of:

   a. Todd Bowles

   b. Bill Parcells

c. Rex Ryan

d. Al Groh

10. The New York Jets and the New England Patriots compete for the right to hold the:

a. AFC East Cup

b. Northeast Trophy

c. Meadowlands Cup

d. Borderline Bowl

11. The New York Jets have a historical rivalry with the Oakland Raiders, which includes the infamous "Heidi Game." Which year did this game take place?

a. 1967

b. 1968

c. 1969

d. 1970

12. The New York Jets and the Miami Dolphins have a tradition of playing an annual game on which holiday?

a. Thanksgiving

b. Christmas

c. New Year's Day

d. Labor Day

13. The New York Jets' rivalry with the New England Patriots intensified during the tenure of which quarterback?

　a. Joe Namath

　b. Chad Pennington

　c. Vinny Testaverde

　d. Mark Sanchez

14. The New York Jets and the New England Patriots have a history of competing in pivotal playoff matchups, including the "New York Sack Exchange" era. Which year did this era peak?

　a. 1978

　b. 1982

　c. 1986

　d. 1992

15. The New York Jets and the Buffalo Bills play for the "Empire Cup" in their annual clash for supremacy in:

    a. New York State

    b. AFC East

    c. Rust Belt Region

    d. Great Lakes Division

16. The New York Jets and the New England Patriots compete in the "Border War" for territorial dominance in the:

    a. AFC East

    b. Northeast Corridor

    c. Tri-State Area

    d. Eastern Seaboard

17. The New York Jets and the Miami Dolphins have a storied rivalry that dates back to the AFL days. What is the nickname for their matchups?

    a. Aqua and Green Feud

    b. Jetstream Showdown

    c. Orange Bowl Brawl

    d. Broadway Beatdown

18. The New York Jets' rivalry with the New England Patriots is characterized by the competitive coaching relationship between:

   a. Bill Belichick and Bill Parcells

   b. Rex Ryan and Eric Mangini

   c. Todd Bowles and Adam Gase

   d. Herm Edwards and Al Groh

19. The New York Jets and the Buffalo Bills have a longstanding rivalry, and their matchups are often referred to as:

   a. Niagara Clash

   b. Lake Erie Brawl

   c. Hudson River Rumble

   d. Erie Canal Classic

20. The New York Jets and the New England Patriots compete for the "Meadowlands Trophy" in recognition of their shared history in:

   a. New York

   b. New Jersey

   c. Connecticut

d. Massachusetts

21. The New York Jets and the Miami Dolphins have a tradition of playing a late-season game known as the:

a. Atlantic Aerial

b. December Duel

c. Winter Warfare

d. Snowbird Shootout

22. The New York Jets and the New England Patriots compete for the "Broadway Bowl" in their annual clashes for supremacy in:

a. New York City

b. AFC East

c. Gillette Stadium

d. Meadowlands

23. The New York Jets' rivalry with the New England Patriots gained intensity during the tenure of which quarterback known for his "Butt Fumble"?

a. Joe Namath

b. Mark Sanchez

c. Chad Pennington

d. Vinny Testaverde

24. The New York Jets and the Miami Dolphins have a tradition of playing a Thanksgiving game known as the:

a. Turkey Tussle

b. Holiday Huddle

c. Miami Mayhem

d. J-E-T-S Feast

25. The New York Jets and the Buffalo Bills have a rivalry that extends beyond football and is often associated with:

a. Baseball

b. Basketball

c. Hockey

d. Soccer

26. The New York Jets and the New England Patriots have a divisional rivalry that often determines the:

a. AFC East Champion

b. Wild Card Spot

c. Super Bowl Winner

d. Pro Bowl Participants

27. The New York Jets and the New England Patriots compete for the "Parcells Trophy" in honor of their shared history with coach:

a. Bill Parcells

b. Rex Ryan

c. Todd Bowles

d. Eric Mangini

28. The New York Jets' rivalry with the New England Patriots is characterized by memorable moments, including the "Duel in the:

a. Meadowlands"

b. Foxborough"

c. Gillette"

d. Northeast"

29. The New York Jets and the Miami Dolphins have a rivalry that often features battles between:

a. Rookie Quarter

backs

b. Elite Receivers

c. Stout Defenses

d. Legendary Coaches

30. The New York Jets and the New England Patriots have a rivalry that has been fueled by controversies, including the "Spygate" scandal involving:

a. Bill Belichick

b. Tom Brady

c. Robert Kraft

d. Wes Welker

ANSWERS

1. c
2. c
3. c
4. a
5. c
6. b
7. b
8. c
9. c
10. a
11. c
12. b
13. d
14. c
15. a
16. c
17. c
18. a
19. d

20. b

21. b

22. a

23. b

24. a

25. c

26. a

27. a

28. a

29. b

30. a

COACHING LEGENDS
QUESTION TIME!

1. Who is considered the coaching legend for the New York Yankees, winning numerous World Series championships?

   a. Joe Torre

   b. Casey Stengel

   c. Yogi Berra

   d. Billy Martin

2. Which coach led the New York Knicks to their only two NBA championships in 1970 and 1973?

   a. Jeff Van Gundy

   b. Red Holzman

   c. Pat Riley

   d. Mike D'Antoni

3. Tom Coughlin is a coaching legend associated with which New York football team?

   a. New York Jets

   b. Buffalo Bills

c. New York Giants

d. New York Titans

4. Who coached the New York Mets to their dramatic World Series victory in 1969?

a. Gil Hodges

b. Davey Johnson

c. Bobby Valentine

d. Yogi Berra

5. Which legendary coach led the New York Giants to victories in Super Bowl XXI and XXV?

a. Bill Parcells

b. Tom Landry

c. Vince Lombardi

d. Bill Belichick

6. The New York Rangers won the Stanley Cup in 1994 under the coaching leadership of:

a. Mike Keenan

b. John Tortorella

c. Herb Brooks

d. Alain Vigneault

7. Who is known as "The Teflon Coach" for his ability to bounce back and succeed after setbacks with the New York Jets?

   a. Rex Ryan

   b. Bill Parcells

   c. Joe Walton

   d. Herman Edwards

8. Which coach led the New York Islanders to four consecutive Stanley Cup championships from 1980 to 1983?

   a. Barry Trotz

   b. Al Arbour

   c. Jack Capuano

   d. Peter Laviolette

9. Who was the head coach of the New York Knicks during the "Linsanity" era in 2012?

   a. Mike Woodson

   b. Jeff Hornacek

c. Mike D'Antoni

d. Larry Brown

10. Which coach guided the New York Giants to a victory in Super Bowl XLII, defeating the undefeated New England Patriots?

a. Tom Coughlin

b. Bill Parcells

c. Jim Fassel

d. Dan Reeves

11. Who served as the head coach of the New York Yankees for 12 seasons, leading the team to six World Series titles?

a. Billy Martin

b. Joe Torre

c. Casey Stengel

d. Joe McCarthy

12. Which coach was behind the bench for the New York Knicks during the infamous "Charles Oakley incident" at Madison Square Garden?

a. Jeff Van Gundy

b. Pat Riley

c. Derek Fisher

d. Mike Woodson

13. Who coached the New York Giants to a victory in Super Bowl XLVI against the New England Patriots?

    a. Tom Coughlin

    b. Bill Parcells

    c. Jim Fassel

    d. Dan Reeves

14. Which coach led the New York Jets to their only Super Bowl victory in 1969?

    a. Weeb Ewbank

    b. Joe Walton

    c. Herm Edwards

    d. Al Groh

15. Who is the winningest coach in New York Giants history, with two Super Bowl victories?

    a. Bill Parcells

    b. Tom Coughlin

c. Jim Fassel

d. Dan Reeves

16. Which coach led the Brooklyn Dodgers to their first and only World Series title in 1955?

a. Walter Alston

b. Leo Durocher

c. Chuck Dressen

d. Casey Stengel

17. Who was the head coach of the New York Knicks during the "Ewing era" in the 1990s?

a. Red Holzman

b. Pat Riley

c. Jeff Van Gundy

d. Mike D'Antoni

18. Which coach was at the helm of the New York Rangers during their 1994 Stanley Cup victory?

a. Mike Keenan

b. John Tortorella

c. Herb Brooks

d. Alain Vigneault

19. Who coached the New York Giants to their first-ever Super Bowl victory in 1987?

a. Bill Parcells

b. Ray Perkins

c. Dan Reeves

d. Jim Fassel

20. The New York Yankees won four World Series titles under the coaching leadership of:

a. Joe Torre

b. Billy Martin

c. Joe McCarthy

d. Casey Stengel

21. Which coach led the New York Knicks to the NBA Finals in 1999 as the eighth seed but lost to the San Antonio Spurs?

a. Jeff Van Gundy

b. Pat Riley

c. Larry Brown

d. Don Nelson

22. Who was the head coach of the New York Jets during the "Broadway Joe" Namath era?

a. Weeb Ewbank

b. Lou Holtz

c. Walt Michaels

d. Rex Ryan

23. Which coach led the New York Giants to a Super Bowl victory in 1990?

a. Bill Parcells

b. Ray Handley

c. Dan Reeves

d. Jim Fassel

24. The New York Rangers won the Stanley Cup in 1940 under the coaching leadership of:

a. Lester Patrick

b. Frank Boucher

c. Lynn Patrick

d. Fred Shero

25. Who coached the New York Knicks during their 1973 NBA championship season?

   a. Red Holzman

   b. Lenny Wilkens

   c. Phil Jackson

   d. Pat Riley

26. Which coach led the New York Giants to victory in Super Bowl XXV against the Buffalo Bills?

   a. Bill Parcells

   b. Ray Handley

   c. Dan Reeves

   d. Bill Belichick

27. Who is known for leading the "Miracle on Ice" U.S. hockey team to victory in the 1980 Winter Olympics and later coached the New York Rangers?

   a. Herb Brooks

   b. Mike Keenan

   c. Alain Vigneault

   d. John Tortorella

28. Which coach led the New York Giants to victory in Super Bowl XLVI against the New England Patriots?

    a. Tom Coughlin

    b. Bill Parcells

    c. Jim Fassel

    d. Dan Reeves

29. Who was the first head coach of the New York Mets when the team was established in 1962?

    a. Yogi Berra

    b. Gil Hodges

    c. Casey Stengel

    d. Joe Torre

30. Which coach led the New York Knicks to the NBA Finals in 1972 and 1973?

    a.

Red Holzman

    b. Pat Riley

    c. Willis Reed

d. Lenny Wilkens

ANSWERS

1. b

2. b

3. c

4. a

5. a

6. a

7. b

8. b

9. a

10. a

11. c

12. a

13. a

14. a

15. b

16. a

17. c

18. a

19. a

20. a

21. a

22. a

23. a

24. a

25. a

26. a

27. a

28. a

29. c

30. a

JETS IN THE PLAYOFFS
QUESTION TIME!

1. In what year did the New York Jets make their first playoff appearance?

   a. 1965

   b. 1968

   c. 1972

   d. 1975

2. The New York Jets won their first Super Bowl by defeating which team in the playoffs?

   a. Dallas Cowboys

   b. Green Bay Packers

   c. Baltimore Colts

   d. Kansas City Chiefs

3. Who was the head coach of the New York Jets during their Super Bowl III victory?

   a. Weeb Ewbank

   b. Lou Holtz

c. Bill Parcells

d. Herm Edwards

4. The New York Jets' quarterback who famously guaranteed a victory in Super Bowl III was:

a. Joe Namath

b. Richard Todd

c. Ken O'Brien

d. Vinny Testaverde

5. In which year did the New York Jets make their most recent playoff appearance before 2021?

a. 2010

b. 2011

c. 2012

d. 2013

6. Who holds the record for the most career playoff touchdown passes as a New York Jets quarterback?

a. Joe Namath

b. Chad Pennington

c. Mark Sanchez

d. Vinny Testaverde

7. The New York Jets' first-round pick in the 2009 NFL Draft, quarterback Mark Sanchez, led the team to consecutive AFC Championship games in which seasons?

   a. 2009 and 2010

   b. 2010 and 2011

   c. 2011 and 2012

   d. 2012 and 2013

8. The New York Jets' memorable playoff victory over the heavily favored Colts in Super Bowl III took place in which city?

   a. Miami

   b. New Orleans

   c. Baltimore

   d. Los Angeles

9. Who is the all-time leading rusher in New York Jets playoff history?

   a. Curtis Martin

   b. Freeman McNeil

c. Thomas Jones

d. Shonn Greene

10. The New York Jets made a miraculous comeback in the 1986 playoffs against the Miami Dolphins, a game often referred to as the "Mud Bowl." Where was this game played?

    a. Shea Stadium

    b. MetLife Stadium

    c. Orange Bowl

    d. Astrodome

11. Which team did the New York Jets defeat in the AFC Championship Game to advance to Super Bowl III?

    a. Oakland Raiders

    b. Kansas City Chiefs

    c. Pittsburgh Steelers

    d. Miami Dolphins

12. The New York Jets' historic win in Super Bowl III was played at:

    a. Tulane Stadium

b. Cotton Bowl

c. Rose Bowl

d. Orange Bowl

13. Who was the head coach of the New York Jets when they made their most recent appearance in the AFC Championship Game in the 2010 season?

   a. Rex Ryan

   b. Eric Mangini

   c. Todd Bowles

   d. Herm Edwards

14. The New York Jets made the playoffs for the first time in franchise history during which season?

   a. 1964

   b. 1968

   c. 1971

   d. 1973

15. In the "Mud Bowl" playoff game in 1986, the New York Jets faced off against the:

   a. Miami Dolphins

b. New England Patriots

c. Cleveland Browns

d. Buffalo Bills

16. Who was the head coach of the New York Jets during their playoff run in the 2009 and 2010 seasons?

a. Rex Ryan

b. Eric Mangini

c. Todd Bowles

d. Herm Edwards

17. The New York Jets defeated the New England Patriots in the 2010 AFC Divisional Round with a game-winning field goal by which kicker?

a. Nick Folk

b. Jay Feely

c. Mike Nugent

d. Doug Brien

18. The New York Jets' first-ever playoff victory occurred against which team?

a. Oakland Raiders

b. Kansas City Chiefs

c. Buffalo Bills

d. Baltimore Colts

19. In the 1998 AFC Championship Game, the New York Jets lost to which team in a heartbreaking overtime defeat?

a. Denver Broncos

b. Tennessee Titans

c. Pittsburgh Steelers

d. Indianapolis Colts

20. Who was the head coach of the New York Jets during their playoff appearance in the 1998 season?

a. Bill Parcells

b. Al Groh

c. Herman Edwards

d. Rich Kotite

21. The New York Jets' first playoff victory in the Super Bowl era came against the:

a. Oakland Raiders

b. Miami Dolphins

c. Baltimore Colts

d. Kansas City Chiefs

22. The New York Jets defeated the Cincinnati Bengals in the 2009 AFC Wild Card Game with a standout performance by which rookie quarterback?

   a. Mark Sanchez

   b. Geno Smith

   c. Chad Pennington

   d. Joe Namath

23. In the 2004 AFC Divisional Round, the New York Jets defeated the San Diego Chargers with a dramatic game-winning field goal by which kicker?

   a. Doug Brien

   b. Mike Nugent

   c. Jay Feely

   d. Nick Folk

24. Who was the head coach of the New York Jets during their playoff appearance in the 2004 season?

a. Eric Mangini

b. Herm Edwards

c. Al Groh

d. Bill Parcells

25. The New York Jets' playoff victory against the New England Patriots in the 2010 season is often remembered for which play?

a. The "Butt Fumble"

b. The "Helmet Catch"

c. The "Immaculate Reception"

d. The "Music City Miracle"

26. Which team did the New York Jets defeat in the 2002 AFC Wild Card Game to secure their first playoff victory in the new millennium?

a. Indianapolis Colts

b. Miami Dolphins

c. San Diego Chargers

d. Oakland Raiders

27. The New York Jets' most recent playoff victory occurred in the 2010 season against which team?

   a. New England Patriots

   b. Pittsburgh Steelers

   c. Indianapolis Colts

   d. Cincinnati Bengals

28. In the 2004 AFC Wild Card Game, the New York Jets defeated which team to advance in the playoffs?

   a. San Diego Chargers

   b. Miami Dolphins

   c. Indianapolis Colts

   d. Cincinnati Bengals

29. The New York Jets made a playoff run in the 1982 season, culminating in a loss to the Miami Dolphins in the AFC Championship Game. What was unique about the 1982 NFL season?

   a. Strike-Shortened Season

   b. Expanded Playoff Format

   c. Neutral

-Site Super Bowl

    d. Rookie Quarterback Showcase

30. Who was the starting quarterback for the New York Jets in their most recent playoff appearance in the 2021 season?

    a. Sam Darnold

    b. Joe Flacco

    c. Zach Wilson

    d. Josh McCown

ANSWERS

1. b
2. c
3. a
4. a
5. d
6. c
7. a
8. c
9. a
10. a
11. a
12. a
13. a
14. c
15. c
16. a

17. a

18. a

19. a

20. a

21. c

22. a

23. a

24. a

25. a

26. a

27. a

28. a

29. a

30. c

COMMUNITY ENGAGEMENT
QUESTION TIME!

1. What is the primary goal of community engagement?

   a. Profit generation

   b. Building strong communities

   c. Political dominance

   d. Environmental preservation

2. Which of the following is an example of community engagement?

   a. Hosting a charity event

   b. Exclusive business partnerships

   c. Closed-door government meetings

   d. Corporate tax evasion

3. In community development, what does the term "empowerment" generally refer to?

   a. Giving power and resources to the community

   b. Centralizing power within the government

   c. Restricting community input

d. Ignoring community needs

4. What role can technology play in community engagement?

   a. Isolating communities

   b. Facilitating communication and collaboration

   c. Decreasing access to information

   d. Promoting exclusion

5. Which of the following is an example of a grassroots community initiative?

   a. Top-down government program

   b. Corporate-sponsored event

   c. Resident-led neighborhood clean-up

   d. Exclusive private club

6. What is the importance of inclusivity in community engagement?

   a. It hinders progress

   b. It fosters diversity and representation

   c. It promotes elitism

   d. It limits community participation

7. What does the acronym NIMBY stand for in the context of community engagement?

   a. New Initiative for Municipal Bylaws

   b. Not In My Backyard

   c. Neighborhood Involvement Management Bureau

   d. National Infrastructure Maintenance and Beautification

8. Which of the following is an example of a community engagement platform?

   a. Exclusive members-only club

   b. Social media platform

   c. Closed-door government meeting

   d. Private business convention

9. How can participatory budgeting contribute to community engagement?

   a. By concentrating decision-making power in government

   b. By involving residents in the budgeting process

   c. By excluding community input

d. By implementing authoritarian financial policies

10. What is the role of community organizers in community engagement?

    a. Isolating communities

    b. Facilitating collaboration and advocacy

    c. Suppressing community voices

    d. Prioritizing corporate interests

11. Which of the following is an example of a civic engagement activity?

    a. Participating in a local election

    b. Ignoring community issues

    c. Excluding certain demographics

    d. Promoting apathy

12. How can community engagement contribute to social cohesion?

    a. By fostering division and conflicts

    b. By encouraging collaboration and understanding

    c. By promoting exclusivity

    d. By ignoring community needs

13. In the context of community engagement, what does the term "bottom-up" approach mean?

　a. Centralized decision-making

　b. Power concentrated at the top levels of government

　c. Initiatives and input coming from the community

　d. Ignoring community feedback

14. Which of the following is an example of a barrier to community engagement?

　a. Open communication channels

　b. Inclusive decision-making processes

　c. Limited access to information

　d. Strong community networks

15. What is the significance of public forums in community engagement?

　a. To limit public discourse

　b. To provide exclusive spaces for certain groups

　c. To facilitate open dialogue and discussion

　d. To suppress community voices

16. How can community engagement contribute to sustainable development?

    a. By disregarding environmental concerns

    b. By promoting short-term economic gains

    c. By involving the community in decision-making for long-term benefits

    d. By focusing solely on corporate interests

17. What is the role of community feedback in the planning process?

    a. It is irrelevant and should be ignored

    b. It provides valuable insights and perspectives

    c. It hinders progress

    d. It is limited to specific demographics

18. How can cultural competence enhance community engagement efforts?

    a. By promoting cultural insensitivity

    b. By excluding diverse perspectives

    c. By fostering understanding and inclusivity

    d. By reinforcing cultural stereotypes

19. Which of the following is an example of a community development project?

    a. A high-end luxury condominium development

    b. A community garden in a public park

    c. An exclusive private golf club

    d. A gated community

20. What role can education play in promoting community engagement?

    a. It can hinder community involvement

    b. It can empower individuals and foster informed participation

    c. It can limit access to information

    d. It can encourage exclusivity

21. What is the purpose of a needs assessment in community engagement?

    a. To ignore community needs

    b. To identify and prioritize community needs

    c. To exclude certain demographics

    d. To promote corporate interests

22. How can social media platforms be utilized for community engagement?

   a. By restricting access to information

   b. By promoting exclusivity

   c. By facilitating communication and information sharing

   d. By isolating communities

23. What is the role of transparency in effective community engagement?

   a. To limit access to information

   b. To promote exclusivity

   c. To foster open communication and trust

   d. To discourage community involvement

24. In community engagement, what does the term "gentrification" refer to?

   a. Preservation of cultural diversity

   b. Economic development without displacement

   c. Displacement of lower-income residents due to wealthier individuals moving in

d. Inclusive community planning

25. How can businesses contribute to community engagement efforts?

a. By prioritizing profit over community needs

b. By engaging in philanthropy and supporting local initiatives

c. By excluding community voices

d. By promoting exclusivity

26. Which of the following is an example of an environmental justice initiative in community engagement?

a. Ignoring pollution concerns in marginalized neighborhoods

b. Prioritizing industrial development without regulation

c. Advocating for clean air and water in all communities

d. Excluding certain demographics from environmental discussions

27. What role can youth engagement play in community development?

   a. Limiting the perspectives brought into the community

   b. Fostering new ideas and energy for positive change

   c. Ignoring the needs of the younger population

   d. Promoting exclusivity

28. What is the purpose of a community needs assessment?

   a. To disregard community needs

   b. To identify and prioritize community needs

   c. To exclude certain demographics

   d. To promote corporate interests

29. How can participatory planning enhance community engagement?

   a. By centralizing decision-making

   b. By excluding community input

   c. By involving residents in the planning process

d. By promoting top-down approaches

30. What is the significance of ongoing communication in community engagement?

a. To limit community involvement

b. To promote exclusivity

c. To foster trust, collaboration, and sustained community involvement

d. To discourage community feedback

ANSWERS

1. b
2. a
3. a
4. b
5. c
6. b
7. b
8. b
9. a
10. c
11. a
12. b
13. c
14. c
15. c

16. c

17. b

18. c

19. b

20. b

21. b

22. c

23. c

24. c

25. b

26. c

27. b

28. b

29. c

30. c

FUTURE PROSPECTS
QUESTION TIME!

1. Which position is often considered the most crucial for a football team's future success?

   a. Wide Receiver

   b. Offensive Lineman

   c. Quarterback

   d. Cornerback

2. The success of an NFL team is closely tied to the performance of:

   a. Special Teams

   b. Defense

   c. Offense

   d. Coaching Staff

3. A team's ability to attract top-tier free agents is influenced by:

   a. Stadium Capacity

   b. Recent Draft Picks

   c. Financial Flexibility

   d. Fan Base Size

4. The long-term success of a team is often tied to the effectiveness of:

   a. Short-Term Strategies

   b. Coaching Staff

   c. Marketing Campaigns

   d. Social Media Presence

5. Which factor is crucial for a team's success in the salary cap era of the NFL?

   a. Attracting Sponsors

   b. Skilled Negotiation in Contracts

   c. Player Popularity

   d. International Fan Base

6. The NFL Draft is an opportunity for teams to:

a. Trade Coaches

   b. Sign Free Agents

   c. Acquire Young Talent

   d. Release Veteran Players

7. In the NFL, a team's schedule is influenced by:

   a. Previous Season's Record

   b. Popularity of the Team

   c. Geographic Location

   d. Player Injuries

8. Which factor plays a significant role in a team's ability to perform well in critical moments, such as playoffs?

   a. Regular Season Record

   b. Team Chemistry

   c. Fan Attendance

   d. Player Endorsements

9. The quality of a team's training facilities and medical staff can impact:

   a. Ticket Sales

b. Player Endorsements

c. Injury Prevention and Recovery

d. Social Media Presence

10. The overall success of an NFL team is influenced by the:

a. Ability to Generate Revenue

b. Number of Social Media Followers

c. Number of International Players

d. Team's Mascot

11. In the context of the NFL, what does the term "rebuilding phase" typically refer to?

a. Focusing on Short-Term Goals

b. Strategically Acquiring Young Talent

c. Relocating the Team

d. Changing the Team's Name

12. A team's future prospects are often linked to the effectiveness of the:

a. Offensive Coordinator

b. General Manager

c. Public Relations Team

d. Stadium Maintenance Crew

13. The use of analytics and data-driven decision-making can positively impact a team's:

   a. Merchandise Sales

   b. Player Contracts

   c. Social Media Engagement

   d. Win-Loss Record

14. The NFL's collective bargaining agreement (CBA) influences:

   a. Ticket Prices

   b. Player Salaries and Benefits

   c. Game Time Schedule

   d. Social Media Policies

15. In the NFL, the term "franchise quarterback" refers to a quarterback who:

   a. Has the most touchdown passes

   b. Has been with the team for the longest period

c. Is considered a long-term solution and leader for the team

d. Has the highest jersey sales

16. The impact of fan support on a team's performance is often referred to as:

a. Home Field Advantage

b. Social Media Buzz

c. Marketing Power

d. Season Ticket Sales

17. The NFL's international series, where games are played outside the United States, aims to:

a. Increase Player Salaries

b. Expand the League's Global Presence

c. Reduce Travel Costs

d. Attract More Sponsors

18. A team's ability to adapt to rule changes and innovations can affect its:

a. Uniform Design

b. Win-Loss Record

c. Popularity on Social Media

d. Fan Base Demographics

19. The utilization of advanced scouting techniques and technology can impact a team's:

   a. Ticket Prices

   b. Draft Position

   c. Social Media Following

   d. Player Injuries

20. The NFL's revenue-sharing model aims to:

   a. Promote Team Rivalries

   b. Ensure Financial Fairness Among Teams

   c. Encourage Teams to Relocate

   d. Increase Player Salaries

21. In the NFL, a team's ability to create a winning culture is often attributed to:

   a. High-Profile Endorsements

   b. Team Traditions and Values

   c. Celebrity Ownership

d. Frequent Coaching Changes

22. A team's approach to community engagement and philanthropy can impact its:

a. Social Media Presence

b. Player Salaries

c. Fan Base Loyalty

d. Tax Deductions

23. The implementation of fan-friendly initiatives, such as interactive stadium experiences, can influence a team's:

a. Social Media Following

b. Player Injuries

c. Merchandise Sales

d. Game Strategy

24. The introduction of new team branding, logos, and uniforms can impact a team's:

a. Player Salaries

b. Fan Base Demographics

c. Social Media Presence

d. Ticket Prices

25. A team's success in the red zone (scoring when close to the opponent's goal line) is often attributed to:

   a. Quarterback's Arm Strength

   b. Defensive Strategies

   c. Offensive Line Performance

   d. Fan Attendance

26. The NFL's emphasis on player safety and rule changes aims to:

   a. Increase Ticket Prices

   b. Reduce Player Salaries

   c. Minimize Injuries and Enhance Longevity

   d. Promote Aggressive Gameplay

27. A team's ability to navigate challenges, such as injuries and suspensions, can impact its:

   a. Social Media Presence

   b. Win-Loss Record

   c. Merchandise Sales

   d. Fan Base Demographics

28. The NFL's partnership with streaming platforms for broadcasting games aims to:

   a. Decrease TV Ratings

   b. Increase Ticket Prices

   c. Expand Viewership and Accessibility

   d. Discourage Social Media Engagement

29. The NFL Scouting Combine is a critical event for teams to evaluate:

   a. Fan Engagement Metrics

   b. Player Performances and Skills

   c. Social Media Campaigns

   d. Coaching Strategies

30. A team's success in securing key sponsorships and partnerships is often influenced by its:

   a. Fan Base Size

   b. Stadium Seating Capacity

   c. Social Media Following

   d. Player Salaries

ANSWERS

1. c

2. c

3. c

4. b

5. b

6. c

7. a

8. b

9. c

10. a

11. b

12. b

13. d

14. b

15. c

16. a

17. b

18. b

19. b

20. b

21. b

22. c

23. a

24. b

25. c

26. c

27. b

28. c

29. b

30. c

GRAET PLAYERS IN JETS HISTORY
QUESTION TIME!

1. Who is the all-time leading passer in New York Jets history?

   a. Joe Namath

   b. Ken O'Brien

   c. Chad Pennington

   d. Mark Sanchez

2. Which player holds the record for the most rushing yards in a single season for the New York Jets?

   a. Curtis Martin

   b. Freeman McNeil

   c. Thomas Jones

   d. Bilal Powell

3. The New York Jets won their first and only Super Bowl in which year?

   a. 1968

   b. 1972

   c. 1981

d. 1994

4. Who is the all-time leading receiver in terms of receiving yards for the New York Jets?

    a. Don Maynard

    b. Wesley Walker

    c. Al Toon

    d. Jerricho Cotchery

5. In what round of the NFL Draft was Joe Namath selected by the New York Jets?

    a. 1st

    b. 2nd

    c. 3rd

    d. 4th

6. Which coach led the New York Jets to their only Super Bowl victory?

    a. Bill Parcells

    b. Weeb Ewbank

    c. Rex Ryan

    d. Herm Edwards

7. The New York Jets' home games are played at which stadium?

    a. MetLife Stadium

    b. Yankee Stadium

    c. Giants Stadium

    d. Citi Field

8. Who is known for the famous play in Super Bowl III guaranteeing a victory for the Jets?

    a. Joe Namath

    b. Matt Snell

    c. Don Maynard

    d. Emerson Boozer

9. Which defensive player is known for his iconic sack celebration, "the airplane"?

    a. Mark Gastineau

    b. Joe Klecko

    c. Shaun Ellis

    d. Muhammad Wilkerson

10. The New York Jets joined the NFL as part of the AFL-NFL merger in which year?

   a. 1960

   b. 1965

   c. 1970

   d. 1975

11. Who is the all-time leading scorer (points) in New York Jets history?

   a. Pat Leahy

   b. Nick Folk

   c. Jason Myers

   d. John Hall

12. Which player holds the record for the most interceptions in a single season for the New York Jets?

   a. Darrelle Revis

   b. Aaron Glenn

   c. Antonio Cromartie

   d. Marcus Coleman

13. The New York Jets' team colors are:

a. Green and White

b. Blue and Gold

c. Black and Silver

d. Red and White

14. Who is the youngest head coach in New York Jets history?

a. Todd Bowles

b. Rex Ryan

c. Adam Gase

d. Robert Saleh

15. The New York Jets' first regular-season game was against which team?

a. New England Patriots

b. Buffalo Bills

c. Miami Dolphins

d. Baltimore Colts

16. Which player is nicknamed "Broadway Joe"?

a. Joe Klecko

b. Joe Namath

c. Joe Ferguson

d. Joe McKnight

17. The New York Jets made history by selecting the first overall pick in the 1997 NFL Draft. Who was that player?

    a. Keyshawn Johnson

    b. Vinny Testaverde

    c. James Farrior

    d. Curtis Martin

18. In what year did the New York Jets become the first AFL team to defeat an NFL team in the Super Bowl?

    a. 1967

    b. 1969

    c. 1973

    d. 1978

19. Which quarterback succeeded Joe Namath as the starting quarterback for the New York Jets?

a. Richard Todd

b. Ken O'Brien

c. Pat Ryan

d. Tony Eason

20. The New York Jets' mascot is named:

a. Jaxson de Ville

b. Blitz

c. Fireman Ed

d. Flight Crew

21. Who is the all-time leader in sacks for the New York Jets?

a. Mark Gastineau

b. Shaun Ellis

c. Muhammad Wilkerson

d. Calvin Pace

22. The New York Jets relocated from which city to become the Jets?

a. Los Angeles

b. Baltimore

c. Houston

d. Boston

23. Which player holds the record for the most touchdown receptions in a single season for the New York Jets?

   a. Brandon Marshall

   b. Keyshawn Johnson

   c. Santana Moss

   d. Laveranues Coles

24. The New York Jets' first head coach was:

   a. Weeb Ewbank

   b. Bill Parcells

   c. Rex Ryan

   d. Lou Holtz

25. Which player was known for his memorable 108-yard kickoff return for a touchdown in Super Bowl III?

   a. George Sauer

b. Don Maynard

c. Emerson Boozer

d. Earl Christy

26. What is the name of the New York Jets' fight song?

a. "We're the New York Jets"

b. "Jet Power"

c. "J-E-T-S"

d. "Take 'Em Down"

27. Who is the only New York Jets player to win the NFL MVP award?

a. Joe Namath

b. Curtis Martin

c. Vinny Testaverde

d. Darrelle Revis

28. Which player is known for coining the term "Sack Exchange"?

a. Joe Klecko

b. Mark Gastineau

c. Abdul Salaam

d. Marty Lyons

29. In which year did the New York Jets move to their current home stadium, MetLife Stadium?

   a. 2007

   b. 2009

   c. 2011

   d. 2013

30. Who is the all-time leader in career interceptions for the New York Jets?

   a. Darrelle Revis

   b. Antonio Cromartie

   c. Aaron Glenn

   d. Erik McMillan

ANSWERS

1. a
2. a
3. a
4. a
5. a
6. b
7. a
8. a
9. a
10. c
11. a
12. a
13. a
14. c
15. d
16. b
17. a
18. b
19. a

20. c

21. a

22. d

23. a

24. a

25. c

26. c

27. a

28. b

29. b

30. d

Printed in Great Britain
by Amazon